P9-CQP-884

The Chicken or the Egg?

By Allan Fowler

Consultants:

Robert L. Hillerich, Ph.D., Bowling Green
State University, Bowling Green, Ohio

Mary Nalbandian, Director of Science,
Chicago Public Schools, Chicago, Illinois

Fay Robinson, Child Development Specialist

CHILDRENS PRESS®
CHICAGO

Design by Beth Herman Design Associates

Library of Congress Cataloging-in-Publication Data

Fowler, Allan
    The chicken or the egg? / by Allan Fowler.
      p. cm. –(Rookie read-about science)
    Summary: A brief look at the physical characteristics, breeds, and
  habits of chickens and at how modern poultry farms produce eggs
  and chickens.
    ISBN 0-516-06008-2
    1. Chickens–Juvenile literature. 2. Eggs–Juvenile literature.
  [1. Chickens. 2. Eggs] I. Title. II. Series: Fowler, Allan.
  Rookie read-about science.
  SF487.5.F69 1993
  636.5–dc20   92-35054
                                                                   CIP
                                                                    AC

A long time ago, certain
brightly colored birds lived
in the jungles in faraway Asia.

Then people started keeping them around their homes – because the birds were good to eat. And so were the eggs they laid.

Little by little, those birds changed – until over the years they became the chickens we know today.

Birds that are raised for food – such as chickens, turkeys, ducks, and geese – are known as poultry.

The people who keep
chickens are poultry farmers.

A single poultry farm
may have thousands and
thousands of chickens.

Plymouth Rocks and
Rhode Island Reds are just
two breeds of chickens.

There are many other breeds.

A male chicken is called a
rooster. A female chicken
is called a hen.

All chickens have combs on top of their heads and wattles under their beaks. On a rooster, the comb and wattle are larger.

Roosters crow –
Cock-a-doodle-doo!
Hens cluck.

And baby chickens peep.

Farmers make sure their
chickens get just the right
corn and grains to grow
big and healthy.

18

Some breeds lay eggs with brown shells. Some lay eggs with white shells.

Brown eggs and white eggs taste the same.

A laying hen lays about
five eggs a week.

The eggs you eat are
unfertilized eggs.
That means there are
no baby chicks growing
inside the eggs.

22
22

If an egg is fertilized, the hen sits on it to keep it warm until it hatches.

But on modern poultry farms, fertilized eggs are put in incubators right after they are laid.

Think about how hot it is on a very hot summer day. It is always like that in an incubator.

After three weeks, the egg hatches.

The baby chick pecks its
way out of the shell.

It is wet and tired. But, after a nap, it is ready to feed itself and to start growing up.

If anyone asks you,
"Which came first, the
chicken or the egg?" –
here's one answer you
can give: "The egg!

Because we eat eggs for
breakfast – and chicken
for dinner."

Words You Know

chickens

comb/wattle

eggs/hatch

chicks

30

poultry farmer

hen

rooster

Plymouth Rock

Rhode Island Red

Index

Asia, 3
baby chicks, 15, 20, 26-27, 30
beaks, 13
breeds of chickens, 10-11, 19
chickens, 5, 6, 7, 8, 9, 10, 12, 13, 14, 15, 16, 28, 30
cluck, 14
combs, 13, 30
corn, 16
crow, 14
ducks, 6
eggs, 4, 19, 20, 23, 24, 28, 30
female chicken, 12
geese, 6
grains, 16

hatching, 23, 24, 30
hen, 12, 14, 20, 23, 31
incubators, 23, 24
jungles, 3
male chicken, 12
peep, 15
Plymouth Rocks, 10, 31
poultry, 6
poultry farmers, 8, 16, 31
poultry farms, 9, 23
Rhode Island Reds, 10, 31
rooster, 12, 13, 14, 31
shells, 19, 26
turkeys, 6
wattles, 13, 30

About the Author

Allan Fowler is a free-lance writer with a background in advertising. Born in New York, he lives in Chicago now and enjoys traveling.

Photo Credits